Question Time

Birds

Angela Wilkes

KING*fisher*

NEW YORK

Editors: Russell Mclean, Jonathan Stroud
Designer: Catherine Goldsmith
Consultants: Joyce Pope, Norah Granger
Production Controller: Jo Blackmore
DTP Coordinator: Sarah Pfitzner
Artwork Archivists: Wendy Allison, Steve Robinson
Indexer: Jason Hook
Illustrators: Lisa Alderson 18-19, 24-25; **Richard Draper** 7*tr*;
Chris Forsey 4-5, 4*bl*, 6-7, 20-21, 28-29; **Ray Grinaway** 8-9,
14-15; **Ian Jackson** 16*l*, 16–17; **Terence Lambert** 10-11, 26–27;
Simon Mendez 12-13; **David Wright** 8*l*, 18*bl*, 22–23, 23*tr*.
Cartoons: Ian Dicks
Picture Manager: Jane Lambert
Picture Acknowledgments: 9*tr* BBC Natural History Unit Picture
Library/William Osborn; **10***cl* Ardea London/Clem Haagner; **13***tl*
www.osf.uk.com/Richard & Julia Kemp; **14***cl* www.osf.uk.com/Mark
Jones; **17***tr* www.osf.uk.com/Norbert Wu; **19***bl* NHPA/Mike Lane;
21*tl* www.osf.uk.com/Daniel J. Cox; **21***cr* BBC Natural History Unit
Picture Library/Staffan Widstrand; **22***cl* NHPA/Stephen Dalton;
25*tr* BBC Natural History Unit Picture Library/Cindy Buxton;
27*tr* NHPA/Bill Coster; **29***cl* NHPA/Roger Tidman;
29*cr* Ardea London/John Cancalosi.

*Every effort has been made to trace the copyright
holders of the photographs. The publishers
apologize for any inconvenience caused.*

KINGFISHER
a Houghton Mifflin Company imprint
215 Park Avenue South
New York, New York 10003
www.houghtonmifflinbooks.com

First published in 2002
10 9 8 7 6 5 4 3 2 1

1TR/0502/TIMS/RNB(RNB)/128MA

Copyright © Kingfisher Publications Plc 2002

All rights reserved under International and
Pan-American Copyright Conventions

LIBRARY OF CONGRESS CATALOGING–IN–
PUBLICATION DATA has been applied for.

ISBN 0-7534-5450-5 (HC)
ISBN 0-7534-5462-9 (PB)

Printed in China

CONTENTS

ABOUT this book

Have you ever wondered why a woodpecker pecks wood? Have all your questions about birds answered, and learn other fascinating facts on every information-packed page of this book. Words in **bold** are in the glossary on page 31.

Look and find

claw

All through the book, you will see the **Look and find** symbol. This has the name and picture of a small object that is hidden somewhere on the page. Look carefully to see if you can find it.

Now I know . . .

★ This box contains quick answers to all of the questions.
★ They will help you remember all about the amazing world of birds.

★ Look and find ★
eye

WHAT is a bird?

Birds are the only animals that have feathers. Most birds can fly, and they all have two wings. To help them fly, birds are extremely light. They have **hollow** bones, a covering of feathers, and a lightweight beak instead of teeth. Their smooth, **streamlined** shape makes it easy for them to slip through the air. Like us, birds are **warm-blooded** and breathe air. Unlike us, they lay eggs.

WHY do birds have feathers?

A bird has three different types of feathers. Small, fluffy down feathers lie next to the bird's skin and help keep it warm. Body feathers cover the down feathers and give the bird a streamlined shape. The strong, stiff feathers on a bird's wings and tail are called flight feathers. They fit together tightly, making a smooth surface that helps the bird fly.

Down feather

Body feathers

Flight feathers

Wing feathers

Tail feathers

A bird's tail helps it steer and brake in the air.

4

That's amazing!

A large bird, such as a goose, can have up to 25,000 feathers. Some tiny hummingbirds have less than 1,000!

A swan is so light that it is only one fourth as heavy as a dog of the same size!

Kingfisher

A bird's beak is made of strong, light horn. Horn is a kind of hard skin.

Birds have scaly legs and feet with claws at the ends of their toes.

HOW many kinds of birds are there?

There are about 9,000 different **species**, or kinds, of birds. They come in all shapes and sizes. Some hummingbirds are the same size as a bumblebee, while an ostrich can grow taller than a human. All birds have wings and feathers, even birds that cannot fly, such as the cassowary. Birds are found all over the world. They live in polar regions and in deserts; in hot, steamy rain forests and in backyards.

Cassowary

The cassowary lives in New Guinea and Australia. It has razor-sharp claws to protect itself against attackers.

Now I know . . .

★ Birds are the only animals that have feathers.
★ Feathers are for warmth, streamlining, and flying.
★ There are about 9,000 different types of birds.

HOW do birds fly?

Birds usually fly by flapping their wings. A bird has strong chest muscles to pull its wings up and then bring them down again. The wing feathers push against the air, which moves the bird forward and up. Birds twist their wings to turn in the air. Some birds flap their wings fast and others slowly. Some birds rise up and dip down in the air. Others **glide** or hover.

A jay jumps into the air and flaps its wings to take off.

Jay

As the bird lifts its wings, the feathers spread apart.

That's amazing!

Albatrosses run so fast when they take off and land that they need a special runway in their nesting colony!

Swifts only stop flying and land when they are nesting. They even sleep in midair!

WHY do hummingbirds hover?

Hummingbirds hover so that they can stop in front of flowers and drink the **nectar** inside. They hold their bodies almost upright and beat their tiny wings back and forth so fast that they make a whirring or humming sound. They are the only birds that can fly sideways, forward, and backward.

Ruby-throated hummingbird

Then the jay pulls its wings down hard.

WHICH bird is like a hang glider?

The wandering albatross spends most of its life gliding just above the ocean surface. It has long, narrow wings and can fly for hours without flapping them. Most seabirds glide. They hold their wings out stiffly and use **currents** of air rising up from the surface of the ocean to keep them in the air and carry them along.

Now I know . . .

★ Birds usually fly by flapping their wings up and down.
★ Hummingbirds hover to feed on the nectar inside flowers.
★ An albatross can fly for hours without flapping its wings.

WHAT do lorikeets eat?

Birds' beaks are different shapes depending on what they eat. Lorikeets live in tropical forests where the trees are in bloom all year round. The lorikeets feed on the **pollen** and sweet nectar inside the tree flowers. They have short, strong beaks for tearing off flower petals and buds and brush-tipped tongues for collecting nectar and pollen. They also eat fruit, grasping it firmly in one foot.

Common crossbill

HOW does a crossbill use its beak?

The crossbill has a unique beak, or bill, which crisscrosses at the tip. The bird uses it just like a tool to help it twist apart the scales on pinecones. Then the crossbill hooks out the seeds with its beak or scoops them out with its long tongue. Sometimes it uses its beak to pick bark off of a tree trunk and then catches the insects living underneath.

That's amazing!

Some birds, such as the cattle egret, stand on animals to feed on the insects living in the animal's fur!

A woodpecker's tongue is so long—sometimes even five times the length of its beak!

WHY does a woodpecker peck wood?

A woodpecker uses its powerful beak to drill through the bark of a tree in search of grubs. Then it scoops them out with its long, sticky tongue. It also drums its beak loudly against a tree to attract a **mate** or to warn rival woodpeckers to stay away from its **territory**.

Rainbow lorikeets

Fig

Eucalyptus buds and flowers

Now I know . . .

★ Lorikeets feed on nectar and pollen from tropical tree flowers.
★ A crossbill uses its beak to pick seeds out of pinecones.
★ Woodpeckers drill into trees to find grubs to eat.

WHY do eagles have huge claws?

Eagles are **birds of prey**—they kill other animals for food. An eagle has very good eyesight. It soars high up in the sky, watching the ground below. When the eagle spots **prey**, it swoops down low and swings its feet forward. It grabs the prey in its giant, curved claws, called **talons**. The eagle carries the prey back to its nest where it tears the dead animal apart with its sharp, hooked beak.

WHERE do vultures find their food?

Vultures are **scavengers**, which means they eat only dead animals. They circle high up in the sky until they see a **carcass** and then flock down to the ground. The vultures peck holes in the carcass and stretch their necks inside. Their heads are bald, which helps keep them clean as they eat.

An eagle's talons are its main weapon. Its forward-pointing toes grab the animal, and its back talons kill it.

10

WHEN do owls hunt?

Most owls hunt at night. They eat small animals such as mice and insects. They have big eyes and can see well in low light, and their hearing is so good that they can even find prey in the dark. Owls are silent hunters because their soft wing feathers muffle out any sound when they swoop in for the kill. Usually owls don't tear up their food before they eat it—they swallow it whole. Later they cough up balls of fur and bones called **pellets**.

A barn owl with a vole

Golden eagle

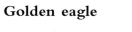

That's amazing!

The peregrine falcon can fly faster than any other bird. It dive-bombs its prey at 125 mph (200km/h)!

Buzzards can spot prey from up to 3 mi. (5km) away!

Owls can't rotate their huge eyes, but they can turn their heads all the way around to see behind them!

Rabbit

Now I know . . .

★ Eagles use their huge talons to catch animals and kill them.
★ Vultures eat dead animals they find on the ground.
★ Owls go hunting for small animals at night.

WHERE do herons stalk?

Wading birds spend most of their time close to ponds, rivers, and marshes where there is always plenty of food. A heron stalks slowly along the edge of the water, looking for fish, frogs, and other small creatures to eat. At the first sign of movement it freezes just like a statue. If an unsuspecting fish swims too close, the heron darts its head forward and snaps up the fish in its long, dagger-shaped beak.

WHY do spoonbills have legs like stilts?

The roseate spoonbill likes to eat small fish, shrimp, and shellfish. It has long, thin legs so that it can wade into water without getting its feathers wet. Its long beak is shaped like two spoons. The spoonbill sweeps its beak from side to side through the water to catch food.

Green-backed heron

Great blue heron

Twelve-spot skimmer dragonfly

A goosander diving for food

HOW do ducks swim and dive?

Most ducks eat water plants and animals, so they swim or dive to reach their food. They have webbed feet set far back on their bodies, which they use like paddles to swim. Some ducks dive underwater to catch fish. They tuck their wings tightly against their body to make themselves streamlined. This means they can swim faster.

The pink color of a spoonbill's feathers comes from shrimp and other small animals it eats.

That's amazing!

The purple gallinule looks like it can walk on water. It actually steps from one lily pad to another!

Sometimes the green-backed heron drops insects into the water as bait to catch fish!

Roseate spoonbill

Great blue heron

Purple gallinule

Now I know . . .

★ Herons stalk along the edge of water in search of food.
★ Spoonbills have long legs so they can wade through water.
★ Ducks have webbed feet like paddles so they can swim well.

WHERE do frigate birds fly?

Frigate birds are fast-flying seabirds. They spend their time soaring over tropical oceans in search of food. Frigates are pirates—they steal from other birds. When they spot birds with fish in their beaks, they chase after them until they drop the food. Frigate birds rarely land on the water but may catch flying fish midair or snatch squid from the sea.

A brown pelican fishing

WHY does a pelican have such a big beak?

Pelicans have long, baggy beaks that stretch to make huge pouches. They use their beaks like fishnets. Brown pelicans dive into the sea and shake their beaks from side to side to scoop up fish. When the pelicans swim back to the surface, they open their beaks a little bit and drain away the water before swallowing their catch.

Frigate bird

That's amazing!

A pelican can hold up to 3 gallons (10L) of water in its beak at once— more than it can hold in its stomach!

When a booby dives for fish, it hits the sea at 60 mph (100km/h)!

14

Frigate birds steal food from tropic birds and other seabirds. They bully them by snapping at their tails as they fly.

A frigate bird has long, powerful wings and a hooked beak for snatching up slippery fish.

Red-billed tropic bird

A blue-footed booby diving for fish

HOW do boobies go fishing?

When a booby spots a **school** of small fish, it dives into the sea like a rocket, pulling back its wings to make them streamlined. The booby plunges several feet below the surface, snaps up fish, and swallows them underwater. Then it returns to the surface to rest for a few minutes.

Herring

Now I know . . .

★ Frigate birds fly over oceans and steal fish from other birds.
★ A pelican uses its beak like a fishnet to scoop up fish.
★ Boobies dive-bomb schools of fish from the air.

15

HOW do ostriches escape danger?

All birds have wings, but they can't all fly. Ostriches are huge flightless birds with long necks and legs. They live on hot, dry grasslands in Africa where there are few places to hide. Because they cannot fly away from **predators** ostriches rely on their speed to escape. Their legs are very strong, and they only have two toes on each foot. This helps them reach speeds of 45 mph (72km/h) in short bursts. They can run at slower speeds for nearly 30 minutes without stopping.

WHERE do kiwis live?

Kiwis are strange, flightless birds that live in the forests of New Zealand. They have small, round bodies and wiry feathers that look like fur. Kiwis live in burrows underground and only come out to feed at night. Unlike other birds, a kiwi has nostrils on the tip of its beak. This helps it sniff for food—earthworms and insects—as it digs around in the dead leaves.

A brown kiwi digging for insects

That's amazing!

Penguins are clumsy walkers. To move fast they slide on their stomachs across the snow like toboggans!

An adult male ostrich is the fastest two-legged runner in the world and can run faster than a racehorse!

Ostriches live in flocks of up to 50 birds, which is safer than being alone.

Ostriches are constantly on the lookout for danger.

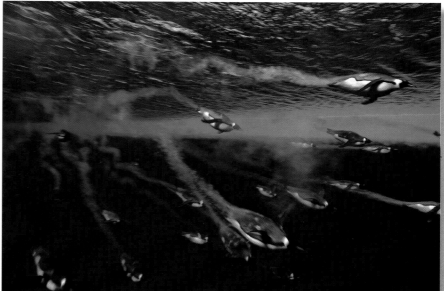

Penguins diving

WHICH bird flies through the water?

Penguins live on the coasts of Antarctica and its islands. They cannot fly—instead they dive into the freezing sea to catch food. A penguin uses its small, stiff wings like flippers to swim underwater and steers with its feet and tail. To go really fast, it clamps its flippers to its sides, making it streamlined. Gentoo penguins can reach speeds of up to 22 mph (36km/h).

Now I know . . .

★ Ostriches are fast runners and can outrun most predators.
★ Kiwis live in burrows in the forests of New Zealand.
★ Penguins cannot fly, but they are very fast swimmers.

Look and find
snake

HOW do macaws recognize each other?

Birds **communicate** with each other using sight and sound. Macaws are colorful parrots that live together in groups in tropical rain forests. Each type of macaw has its own bright colors and markings, kind of like its own uniform. The birds recognize each other by the colors and patterns of their feathers, so they know to which group they belong. Other birds may not be brightly colored, but they have markings on their faces or bodies that help them recognize each other.

WHICH bird changes color?

Many birds use color to hide from enemies. This is called **camouflage**. All birds **molt**—the ptarmigan even molts twice a year, changing color to match the season. In the winter, when snow is on the ground, it has white feathers. In the spring it molts and grows brown feathers that blend in with the land where it lives. When the winter comes, it molts again and grows white feathers.

That's amazing!

The booming call of a bittern can be heard for 3 mi. (5km) across the reed beds where it lives!

The twit-twoo call of a tawny owl is actually made by two birds. One owl calls "twit." and the other replies "twoo!"

Scarlet macaws

Macaws often gather
on riverbanks to eat clay.
This helps them **digest**
the tough seeds they eat.

WHY do birds sing?

Many birds, such as the robin, sing to
send messages to other birds. Each type of
songbird has its own song.
By singing birds show
who they are and claim
a patch all their own.
In the spring many
birds sing together
loudly at dawn. The
sound they make is
known as the dawn chorus.

Now I know . . .

★ Macaws recognize each other
by the colors of their feathers.
★ Molting allows a ptarmigan
to change color twice a year.
★ Birds sing to announce who
they are to other birds.

19

WHY do peacocks show off?

Before a bird can lay eggs it has to find a mate. The females usually do the choosing, so male birds, called peafowls, do their best to impress them. Peafowls are brightly colored and have long, shimmering tail feathers. They open these out like fans and rustle them to show off the tail's "eyes." The females, called peahens, are a dull brown, so they can nest without enemies noticing them. After the birds have mated the peahen builds a nest and raises her chicks all on her own.

That's amazing!

The male frigate bird shows off to females by inflating a huge red pouch below his throat!

Some birds of paradise hang upside down from a branch to impress any females watching!

The peahen pretends to ignore the peafowl, but this is all part of finding a mate.

Peahen

Japanese cranes dancing

WHICH birds dance together?

In some species of birds the males and females look alike. They go through a special **courtship** routine to find a mate. Cranes gather in groups and choose partners by dancing together. They form pairs and then bow, flap their wings, jump into the air, and sing duets. Each pair of birds builds a nest, and both birds take part in raising the chicks.

HOW does a bowerbird win a mate?

A male satin bowerbird builds an avenue of twigs, called a bower, to attract females. He uses the bower to display the treasures he has collected. He lays out berries, feathers, and shells, all colored blue like him. He even smashes berries so he can paint the walls of his bower with blue juice.

Satin bowerbird

Peafowl

Now I know . . .

★ Peafowls show off their beautiful feathers to win a mate.
★ Cranes choose a mate by dancing together.
★ Bowerbirds build courtship bowers to attract females.

21

WHICH bird weaves its nest?

Birds build nests so that they have a safe, sheltered place to lay their eggs and raise their chicks. Many nests are small and cup-shaped, but some weaverbirds in Africa make giant nests by weaving blades of grass together. The male bird weaves a round nest with a long entrance tunnel. He hopes the nest will impress a female enough to mate with him.

A swallow feeding its chicks

The weaverbird starts by making a ring out of grass stems. He builds around this to finish the nest.

WHAT does a swallow use to build its nest?

Swallows build cup-shaped nests out of damp mud and line them with grass or soft feathers. They often build their nests on a ledge or beam inside a barn. Birds build nests out of all kinds of things, from twigs and moss to silk from spiderwebs.

That's amazing!

Some weaverbirds live in enormous nests that cover a whole treetop. The nests may be 100 years old and have 400 birds living in them!

Gannets and boobies keep their eggs warm by standing on them with their big webbed feet!

22

The long entrance tunnel will stop snakes and other enemies from entering the nest and stealing the eggs or eating the chicks.

When the nest is finished, the male hangs upside down from it and flutters his wings to attract a female.

Male weaverbird

WHY do birds sit on eggs?

Birds' eggs have to be **incubated**—kept at just the right temperature—for chicks to grow inside of them. Most birds lay a **clutch** of eggs over a number of days. Once all the eggs have been laid one parent sits on them to keep them warm. Usually the female sits on the eggs, but sometimes the male takes a turn.

Now I know . . .

★ Some weaverbirds make nests woven out of grass.

★ Swallows make their nests from damp mud and grass.

★ Birds sit on eggs to keep them warm so chicks can grow inside.

WHAT do baby birds eat?

Many baby birds are born naked and blind. They cannot walk or fly so their parents feed them. Chicks need huge amounts of body-building food, such as insects, because they grow so fast. The parents fly back and forth all day, dropping food into their gaping beaks. The chicks stay in the nest until their feathers have grown and they can fly away. Even then their parents often continue helping them find food.

That's amazing!

Some cuckoos lay their eggs in other birds' nests. When the cuckoo chick hatches, it pushes the other eggs out of the nest!

A great tit may deliver food to its nest 900 times a day!

The chicks' wide-open beaks are a signal to their parents that they need to be fed.

HOW do chicks hatch?

When a chick is ready to **hatch**, it chips a hole in its eggshell with a sharp point on its beak called an egg tooth. When the hole is big enough, the chick pushes itself out. Ducklings and other birds that nest on the ground have their eyes open when they hatch. They are covered with soft down and can walk immediately.

Ducklings hatching

Grub

Adult blue tit feeding its chicks

WHERE does a shoebill stork raise its chick?

Shoebill storks live on African marshes among tall, thick reeds. They build nests on floating beds of plants and usually have one chick. To feed it, they cough up fish and water snakes that they have already eaten. During the heat of the day the mother shades her chick from the sun and sprinkles big beakfuls of water over it to keep it cool.

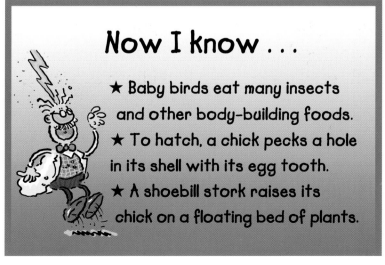

Now I know . . .

★ Baby birds eat many insects and other body-building foods.
★ To hatch, a chick pecks a hole in its shell with its egg tooth.
★ A shoebill stork raises its chick on a floating bed of plants.

WHERE do geese fly in the fall?

Brant geese spend the summer in the far north, where their chicks hatch. But the northern winter is very cold, and food is hard to find, so in the fall the geese fly south. They fly thousands of miles to warmer places where there is plenty of food. The next spring they return to their summer home. These journeys are called **migrations**. Many birds migrate, and some fly all the way without stopping. Others land from time to time to rest and eat before continuing on their way.

Brant geese

Geese migrate in large flocks. They usually fly in a V-shaped group and take turns being leader so none of them become too tired.

That's amazing!

Bar-headed geese fly across the highest mountains in the world to reach their winter homes. They fly nearly as high in the sky as jet planes!

Snow geese can fly nearly 1,865 mi. (3,000km) in just two days!

WHICH bird makes the longest journey?

Arctic terns fly right across the world and back every year. In the late summer they leave the countries around the Arctic Ocean and fly to Antarctica, where the summer is just beginning. In the spring they fly back again. This round trip of 15,535 mi. (25,000km) means they can enjoy the summer all year round.

Arctic tern

Geese honk to each other as they fly to keep in touch with all the other members of the group.

HOW do migrating birds find their way?

Migrating birds follow the same routes every year. They may use the position of the sun and the stars to help them find their way. Also birds often follow familiar features in the landscape below them. They fly along mountain ranges, river valleys, and coastlines.

Now I know . . .

★ Brant geese fly south in the fall to find food in a warmer place.
★ Arctic terns travel the farthest when they migrate.
★ Birds may use the sun and stars to help find their way.

Look and find
beetle

WHY are many birds in danger?

Birds around the world are under threat. Most birds are especially equipped to life in one type of **habitat**, such as forests or marshes. Many of these habitats are being **polluted** or destroyed, so birds are losing their homes and food supplies. Many birds are killed by hunters or are caught and sold as pets. This means that some birds, such as the quetzal of Central America, are in danger of becoming **extinct**.

That's amazing!

Many flightless birds, such as the dodo, died out because they could not fly to escape danger!

At least 1,000 species—about one in nine of the world's bird species—are in danger of extinction.

Resplendent quetzal

WHERE was the takahe saved?

The takahe is a brightly-colored, flightless bird from New Zealand that people thought was extinct. Then in 1948 a small group of takahes was found living in a remote valley. Now **conservationists** are keeping the takahes on a small island where they are safe from predators and hunters. As the takahes breed and have chicks their numbers will increase. This will give them a better chance of survival.

A takahe looking for grass seeds to eat

HOW do oil spills harm birds?

Oil spills at sea kill many seabirds every year. The sticky oil glues their feathers together so the birds can't keep warm, swim, or fly. If a bird swallows oil, it becomes sick. Some people rescue birds and wash their feathers to remove the oil. They keep the birds warm and feed them until they can fly again.

Now I know . . .

★ Many birds are in danger because their habitats are being destroyed.
★ Birds die unless oil from spills is cleaned off of their feathers.
★ The rare takahe is being bred on an island near New Zealand.

29

BIRDS QUIZ

What do you remember about birds? Test what you know, and see how much you have learned.

1 What do hummingbirds like to eat?
a) seeds
b) fruit
c) nectar

2 Which bird has a long, sticky tongue?
a) macaw
b) woodpecker
c) cassowary

3 Which bird feeds on animal carcasses?
a) eagle
b) owl
c) vulture

4 Where do spoonbills live?
a) by water
b) in forests
c) on pack ice

5 Which bird steals food from other birds?
a) pelican
b) frigate bird
c) robin

6 Which bird lives in an underground burrow?
a) blue tit
b) lorikeet
c) kiwi

7 Why does a frigate bird puff out its chest?
a) to go swimming
b) to help it fly
c) to impress female birds

8 Which bird can run faster than a racehorse?
a) ostrich
b) heron
c) penguin

9 Where does a shoebill stork build its nest?
a) on a riverbank
b) on floating plants
c) on a chimney top

10 How does an albatross usually fly?
a) it hovers
b) it glides
c) it flaps its wings fast

Find the answers on page 32.

GLOSSARY

birds of prey Birds that hunt and kill other animals for food.

camouflage Colors, markings, or patterns that help an animal blend in with its background so it is difficult to see.

carcass The dead body of an animal.

clutch A group of eggs laid by a bird and incubated together.

communicate To pass information to others.

conservationists People who help save habitats and animals from being changed, harmed, or ruined.

courtship The special way in which animals behave when they are looking for a mate.

currents Flows of water or air.

digest To break food down into tiny pieces that can be used by the body.

extinct Died out and not existing any more.

glide A bird glides when it sails through the air without flapping its wings.

habitat The natural home of an animal or plant, such as forests, marshes, or grasslands.

hatch To break out of an egg.

hollow Not solid.

incubated Kept warm. Eggs are incubated so that chicks can grow inside them.

mate A partner.

migrations Regular journeys that some animals make from one place to another to nest or find food.

molt To lose old, worn-out feathers (or fur) and grow new ones in their place.

nectar The sweet juice deep inside flowers that some birds and insects like to eat.

pellets Balls of undigested food that some birds cough up.

pollen A sticky, yellow powder made by flowers.

polluted Made dirty and dangerous by oil or waste products.

predators Animals that hunt and kill other animals.

prey Animals that are hunted and killed by other animals.

scavengers Animals that eat only dead or dying animals.

school A large group of fish that swim and feed together.

species A particular type of animal or plant.

streamlined Having a smooth shape that can move easily through air or water.

talons The long, sharp claws of a bird of prey.

territory The area in which an animal lives and finds food.

warm-blooded Having a constant body temperature.

INDEX

Answers to the Birds Quiz on page 30

★ 1 c ★ 2 b ★ 3 c ★ 4 a ★ 5 b ★ 6 c ★ 7 c ★ 8 a ★ 9 b ★ 10 b